A Robbie Reader

Bubonic Plague

Jim Whiting

Mitchell Lane
PUBLISHERS

P.O. Box 196
Hockessin, Delaware 19707
Visit us on the web: www.mitchelllane.com
Comments? email us:
mitchelllane@mitchelllane.com

Mitchell Lane PUBLISHERS

Printing   1   2   3   4   5   6   7   8   9

A Robbie Reader/Natural Disasters

The Ancient Mystery of Easter Island
The Bermuda Triangle
Bubonic Plague
Earthquake in Loma Prieta, California, 1989
The Fury of Hurricane Andrew, 1992
Hurricane Katrina, 2005
The Lost Continent of Atlantis
Mt. Vesuvius and the Destruction of Pompeii, A.D. 79
Mudslide in La Conchita, California, 2005
Tsunami Disaster in Indonesia, 2004
Where Did All the Dinosaurs Go?

Library of Congress Cataloging-in-Publication Data
Whiting, Jim, 1943–
    Bubonic plague / by Jim Whiting.
        p. cm. — (Natural disasters)
    Includes bibliographical references and index.
    ISBN 1-58415-494-2 (library bound)
    1. Plague—Juvenile literature. 2. Plague—History—Juvenile literature. I. Title.
II. Series.
    RC171.W59 2007
    614.5'732—dc22   2006006102

ISBN-10: 1-58415-494-2   ISBN-13: 9781584154945

ABOUT THE AUTHOR: Jim Whiting has been a remarkably versatile and accomplished journalist, writer, editor, and photographer for more than 30 years. A voracious reader since early childhood, Mr. Whiting has written and edited about 200 nonfiction children's books. His subjects range from authors to zoologists and include contemporary pop icons and classical musicians, saints and scientists, emperors and explorers. Representative titles include *The Life and Times of Franz Liszt*, *The Life and Times of Julius Caesar*, *Charles Schulz*, *Charles Darwin and the Origin of the Species*, *Juan Ponce de Leon*, *Annie Oakley*, and *The Scopes Monkey Trial*. He lives in Washington State with his wife and two teenage sons.

PHOTO CREDITS: Cover, p. 1—North Wind Picture Archives; pp. 4, 13—Library of Congress; pp. 8, 11, 12, 20, 26—Center for Disease Control; p. 14—NASA/Goddard Space Flight Center/ORBIMAGE; p. 18—Encyclopedia Britannica; p. 22—Bridgeman Art Library; p. 24—Ted Streshinsky/CORBIS.

PUBLISHER'S NOTE: The following story has been thoroughly researched and to the best of our knowledge represents a true story. While every possible effort has been made to ensure accuracy, the publisher will not assume liability for damages caused by inaccuracies in the data, and makes no warranty on the accuracy of the information contained herein.

To reflect current usage, we have chosen to use the secular era designations BCE ("before the common era") and CE ("of the common era") instead of the traditional designations BC ("before Christ") and AD (*anno Domini*, "in the year of the Lord").

PLB

TABLE OF CONTENTS

Words in **bold** type can be found in the glossary.

Wealthy citizens cover their noses to avoid catching the disease that was killing hundreds in their city of Florence, Italy. By the time the Black Death reached William's village in England, it had already struck other countries in Europe.

A Horrible Way to Die

Life had always been the same for nine-year-old William. He lived in an English village in 1348. His whole family got up early and worked in the fields all day. Then they ate dinner and went to bed.

One fall day, a frightened man hurried through the village. He said a deadly disease had just arrived in England. Other travelers followed. The disease seemed to be getting closer.

Soon afterward, a villager complained of a headache and very sore legs. His body shook with chills. Angry red blotches broke out on his chest. Several swollen lumps on his body grew to the size of eggs. They turned black and then burst. He coughed and sneezed and vomited blood. He tossed and turned in agony. Within four days, he was dead.

By this time, other villagers were sick. They began dying as well. Everyone was very frightened of this mysterious illness.

Many people in the village believed God was punishing them for their sins. William's parents prayed even more than they usually did. They hoped their family would be spared.

It wasn't. William's older brother John became ill. Two days later, his sister Maud was sick, and then Thomas and Henry. The day Henry died, William's father came down with the disease.

William's father was the last villager to die of the Black **Plague** (PLAYG). No one else got sick. The survivors buried their dead friends, relatives, and neighbors.

Someone said more than 200 people lived in the village before the disease struck. When it was over, there were less than 100. William's

Red blotches and ugly black bumps cover the bodies of two plague victims. The doctor behind them tries to protect himself by holding flowers. Many people believed that flowers could prevent or cure the sickness.

mother married a man who had lost his wife. The plague had also claimed three of the man's five children.

For William, life would go on—but he would never forget what happened to his family in the year 1348.

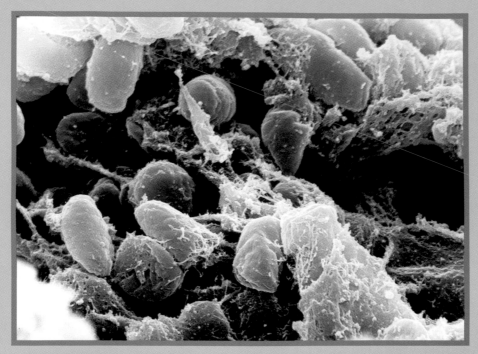

Bubonic plague is caused by bacteria. The top photo shows a magnified view of the bacteria as seen in fluorescent light. The bottom photo shows a magnified view of the bacteria in the bloodstream.

The Mighty Flea

What was this awful disease? Today we call it bubonic plague (boo-BAH-nik PLAYG). The outbreak in the 1300s is known as the Black Death. It is named for the black lumps, or **buboes**, that show up on victims.

Civic officials tried their best to contain the disease. They walled up houses that held sick people. Seaport cities tried to keep crews of incoming ships from going ashore. These measures helped a little, but the disease continued to rage.

It broke many families apart. They didn't want to touch each other. They had good reason. Anyone, even doctors, who came into contact with sick people usually died.

Many bodies were carried to ditches, dumped inside, and hastily covered with dirt. Often corpses lay in the streets for days. The foul odor from all the dead bodies was very strong.

Because of the stink, some people carried fresh flowers. Others burned **incense**. The pleasant smell masked the odor. People hoped it would also keep the disease away. They tried many other tricks to avoid the disease. Some people put their faith in loud noises. They rang church bells or fired cannons to scare away the evil. Sleeping in daytime was discouraged, as was taking baths. A few people even cautioned about the "dangers" of physical exercise.

A number of people simply ran away from their homes. A few managed to escape that way. Others didn't. They eventually caught the disease. For poor people, running away wasn't an option. They had to stay put.

No one guessed what really made the disease spread. It was fleas.

Bacteria (bak-TEER-ee-uh) lived inside the fleas. Some bacteria are important for health. Some bacteria make people sick. This particular bacteria was deadly.

Fleas need a constant supply of blood or they will starve. Fleas carrying the plague bacteria lived on rats. They passed their deadly germs to the rats. The rats quickly died, but the fleas still had to eat. They jumped from dead

This flea (magnified) is full of animal blood. Some fleas lived on blood from rats that were infected with the plague bacteria. If the fleas bit a human, they would pass along the disease.

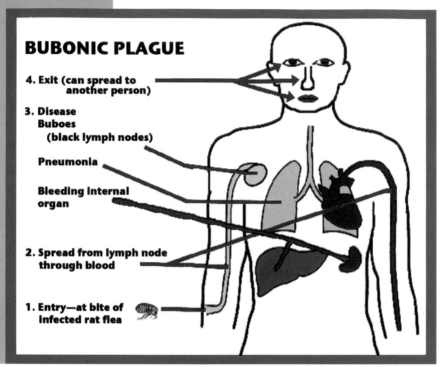

BUBONIC PLAGUE

4. Exit (can spread to
        another person)

3. Disease
    Buboes
        (black lymph nodes)

Pneumonia

Bleeding internal
organ

2. Spread from lymph node
    through blood

1. Entry—at bite of
    infected rat flea

When a disease-carrying flea bit a person, the bacteria would travel to a **lymph node**, which would create black buboes. The bacteria would also spread through the blood, causing body organs to bleed. If the lungs became infected, the person could then spread the bacteria to other people through coughing or sneezing.

rats to nearby humans. One bite from a flea could infect its new host.

The disease spread in another way. When plague victims coughed or sneezed, millions of bacteria went into the air. People nearby could become infected through breathing that air.

Edward III became king in 1327 when he was only 15. He ruled for 50 years until his death in 1377. He was a successful king who enlarged the amount of territory that England controlled. The plague struck his country in the middle of his reign.

Conditions of the times aided in the spread of the disease. Most people didn't eat very healthfully. They were surrounded by filth. **Sanitation** was difficult. Many rivers were polluted. Early in 1349, England's King Edward III complained to the London town council about the city's filthy streets. The council said the problem couldn't be helped. All the street cleaners had died of the plague.

Many people in England hoped that the English Channel would protect them from the disease. It didn't. It is only about 20 miles wide between Dover, England, and Calais, France. Ships would often cross it. Some of those ships carried the plague with them.

The Plague Breaks Out

The outbreak in the 1300s wasn't the only time bubonic plague terrorized the world. It also struck in the sixth and seventeenth centuries. It is estimated that over 75 million people died from these three outbreaks.

Most people believe the Black Death—the outbreak of the fourteenth century—began in central Asia in the late 1320s. A heavily traveled trade route called the **Silk Road** helped the disease to spread from there. Rats and the fleas they carried often crawled into the traders' cargo. These "hitchhikers" brought the disease with them to new locations.

This plague became a pandemic (pan-DEH-mik), which means it spread rapidly and far. Pandemics affect large areas: countries, continents, sometimes even the whole world. In 1333, millions of people in China died from the Black Plague.

The city of Genoa (JEH-noh-uh), Italy, was very prosperous in that era. It set up a **colony** (KAH-luh-nee) called Kaffa (KAH-fah) in southern Russia (modern Feodosiya on the Black Sea). **Mongol** soldiers infected with the plague attacked Kaffa in 1347. The disease spread to the city's inhabitants, and many died.

The survivors fled to Messina, a town on the Italian island of Sicily. They brought the disease with them. It spread through the rest of the island, and then crossed to Italy. From there, it traveled through the rest of Europe. It tended to follow trade routes.

For months, anxious English people heard reports of the horrible plague coming closer and closer. They hoped that the English Channel, which separated their island nation from mainland Europe, might save them. It didn't.

Colonists from Genoa, Italy, were infected by Mongol warriors in 1347. Surviving colonists fled to Messina, spreading the plague through the island of Sicily. From there, the plague made it back to mainland Italy and through the rest of Europe.

When the disease crossed the English Channel, an estimated 6 million people lived in England. At least 2 million of them died. It would take nearly 400 years for the population of England to return to its pre-plague level.

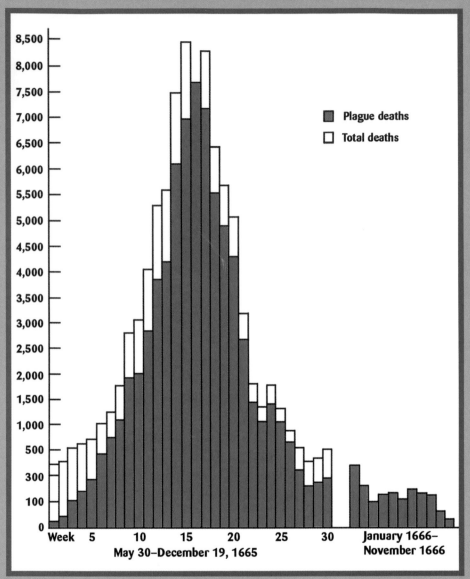

The towering bar graph on the left shows the number of deaths each week from the Great Plague of London. The graph spans 30 weeks, from May 30 to December 19, 1665. The much smaller graph on the right shows the monthly plague deaths from January 1666 to November 1666. Fewer people died in an entire year than in a single week at the peak of this outbreak of the plague.

Reaching Its Peak

For over a hundred years, many youngsters have joined in a circle, linked their arms, and sung this nursery rhyme:

Ring around the rosies
A pocket full of posies,
Ashes, ashes,
We all fall down.

Some people believe that this song originated in England during the Great Plague of 1665. One sign of the disease was a red (rose-colored) splotch on the skin. Many people carried posies (little flowers) with them. They believed that the sweet odor of the flowers would keep the disease from infecting them. In England, kids sing *atichoo!* (sneezing)

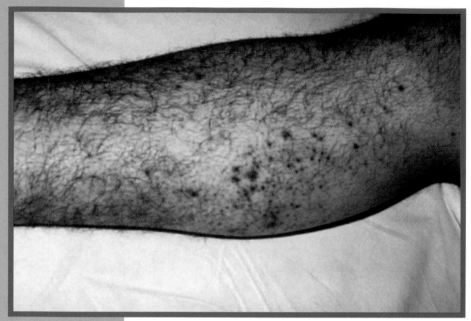

An early sign of bubonic plague is rosy red blotches on the skin. During the Middle Ages, these blotches would signal the beginning of a painful death. In many countries today, this person's chances of survival would be very good.

instead of *ashes.* Plague victims often sneezed or coughed. When people got sick and died, they fell down.

Children in every country in Europe could have sung the same song three centuries earlier. The disease spread slowly but surely throughout the continent.

The Black Death followed trade routes from China to Kaffa, across the Black Sea to Constantinople, and then to Sicily and the rest of Europe. Coastal cities in Africa also suffered.

Some people wrote descriptions of the plague. One of the saddest ends with the sentence, "The plague ended _____." The man who wrote it was going to fill in the date later. The space remains blank. He died during the plague.

By 1351 it crossed into northern Russia. The following spring, it reached the southern

Russian city of Kiev (kee-EV). Kiev was only a few hundred miles from Kaffa. The plague had traveled nearly full-circle around Europe. Scientists estimate that by then it had killed about 20 million people—one of every three people in Europe. Soon thereafter, the rate of new victims decreased. The immediate danger was over.

The Great Fire of London broke out in September 1666. Many authorities believe that it helped bring the Great Plague of 1665 to an end. It burned the rats that carried the disease.

The plague hadn't really gone away. Every few years there would be a fresh outbreak. The outbreaks stayed local, affecting a relatively small area. They still killed many people in those areas, but they didn't become pandemics. For example, in London in 1665, an estimated 75,000 to 100,000 people died of the plague. That was about one-fifth of the city's population. It ended when the Great Fire of London burned much of the city, killing the plague-carrying rats and fleas.

By the end of the seventeenth century, plague had virtually disappeared from Europe—but the disease was still lurking. And its cause was still unknown.

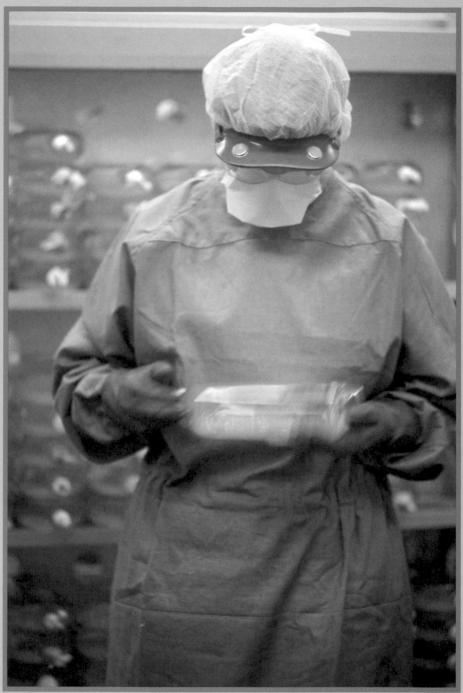

A laboratory worker carefully handles a vaccine used against bubonic plague. The plague bacteria is highly contagious, so the person wears a great deal of protective clothing.

Can the Plague Strike Again?

A new plague pandemic began shortly after 1850. It was centered in Asia. In some areas, it lasted for many years. Millions of people died. Forty years later, scientists finally learned that fleas carried the plague, helping it spread. Once they found the cause, they developed **vaccines** (vak-SEENZ) to help control it.

Today, it is hard for many people to think of such a horrid death, but bubonic plague still exists. It is more likely to appear in remote areas with a lot of small wild animals. Fortunately, very few people in modern times will die of the plague.

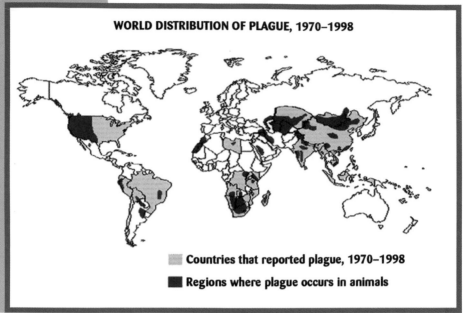

Between 1970 and 1998, the plague was reported in countries around the world. Animals are still carriers of the plague bacteria. In the United States, these animals include prairie dogs, chipmunks, and ground squirrels.

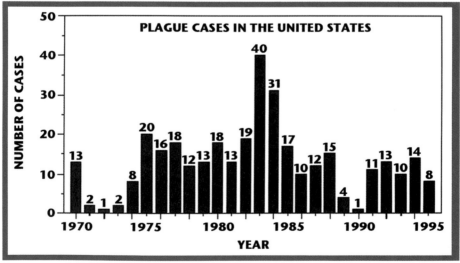

Between 1970 to 1995, there was at least one case of the plague per year in the United States. Most of the victims survived. The death rate in the United States is about one in every seven cases.

There is an important difference between the present era and the middle of the fourteenth century. At that time, the plague took weeks or even months to travel relatively short distances. Since the early 1900s, travel times have become much shorter, so disease can spread more quickly.

The last worldwide disease pandemic began in 1918. It was not the bubonic plague. This disease, called the Spanish flu, killed an estimated 50 million people.

There are still many dangerous germs in the world. A person carrying these germs can travel thousands of miles in a few hours, coming into contact with thousands of people. Scientists and medical researchers have to always be alert for new threats. No one wants another Black Death.

CHRONOLOGY

Late 1320s	Plague begins in central Asia.
1333	Plague strikes China.
1347	Plague appears in Kaffa.
October 1347	Kaffa colonists reach Messina, Sicily, bringing the plague with them.
Spring 1348	Plague arrives in Paris, France.
Fall 1348	Plague comes to England.
1349	Plague reaches Ireland and Norway.
1350	Plague infects eastern Europe.
1351	Plague strikes northern Russia.
Spring 1352	Plague reaches Kiev, Russia. Infection rates begin to decline.

TIMELINE OF OTHER PLAGUES

ca. 1050 BCE	According to the biblical Book of Samuel, plague strikes the Philistines for stealing the Ark of the Covenant. Some scholars believe this plague was the bubonic plague.
430 BCE	Plague kills many people in Athens, Greece, during a war with Sparta. The cause is unknown, but it may have been bubonic plague.
541–542 CE	Plague of Justinian strikes Constantinople and the eastern Mediterranean.
1629–1631	Great Plague of Milan strikes northern Italy.

1664–1665	Great Plague breaks out in London, claiming between 75,000 and 100,000 victims.
1679–1680s	Great Plague of Vienna, Austria, is part of another pandemic.
1855	Third Pandemic breaks out in China and India; it lasts for more than a century. More than 12 million die in China and India alone. It eventually spreads throughout the world. It is regarded as active until 1959, when the death toll around the world finally drops below 200.
1918–1919	Worldwide "Spanish flu" pandemic causes an estimated 50 million deaths. It was a greater killer than any of the outbreaks of bubonic plague.

FIND OUT MORE

Books

Biel, Timothy. *The Black Death*. San Diego: Lucent Books, 1989.

Cefrey, Holly. *The Plague*. New York: The Rosen Publishing Group, 2001.

Day, James. *The Black Death*. New York: Bookwright Press, 1989.

Elliott, Lynne. *Medieval Medicine and the Plague*. New York: Crabtree Publishing Company, 2006.

McGowen, Tom. *The Black Death*. New York: Franklin
    Watts, 1995.
Ward, Brian. *Epidemic*. New York: DK Books, 2000.

Works Consulted
Cantor, Norman F. *In the Wake of the Plague*. New
    York: Perennial, 2002.
Kelly, John. *The Great Mortality: An Intimate History
    of the Black Death, the Most Devastating Plague of
    All Time*. New York: HarperCollins Publishers Inc.,
    2005.
Knox, E.L. Skip. "The Black Death." http://
    history.boisestate.edu/westciv/plague/
Ziegler, Philip. *The Black Death*. New York: Harper
    Torchbooks, 1969.

On the Internet
The Black Death (Bubonic Plague) —History for Kids
http://www.historyforkids.org/learn/medieval/
    history/highmiddle/plague.htm
The Black Death
http://www.insecta-inspecta.com/fleas/bdeath/
    index.html
Disease in the 14th Century
http://www.spartacus.schoolnet.co.uk/
    YALDdisease.htm

GLOSSARY

bacteria (bak-TEER-ee-uh)—Tiny one-celled organisms that can have an effect on much larger organisms such as humans and other animals.

buboes (BOO-bohz)—Badly swollen glands that are a sign of bubonic plague.

colony (KAH-luh-nee)—People from one area who move to a new location but remain under the control of their original government.

incense (IN-sens)—Material that releases a pleasant smell when it is burned.

lymph node (LIMF nohd)—A gland in the body that holds a clear liquid called lymph. Lymph can travel through body tissue and into the blood.

Mongol (MAHN-gul)—A person living in the empire founded by Genghis Khan; its soldiers conquered a great deal of territory in Asia and eastern Europe.

plague (PLAYG)—A widespread disease that kills many people.

sanitation (saa-nih-TAY-shun)—Promoting good health and reducing the possibility of disease by maintaining clean conditions.

Silk Road—A famous trade route that connected China with the Mediterranean Sea.

vaccines (vak-SEENZ)—Substances given to people to decrease their chances of catching a disease.

INDEX